I'm the
Proud
Grandmother

_____

and this book is about

Alicia Jennifer

my No. 1
Grandchild

To Grandma Yaphe,
Merry Christmas
Lots of Love
Alicia

Christmas 1979

Lovingly dedicated to you!
The proud and happy Grandma.

dolli tingle

LOOK WHO'S A GRANDMA!

Written and illustrated by Dolli Tingle

The C. R. Gibson Company
Norwalk, Connecticut

So you are a Grandma!
How perfectly quaint!
Well, never mind, dear,
It's a common complaint.
It won't get you down
If you simply don't let it.
Go buy a new hat!
THAT will help you forget it!

Copyright MCMLXXI by The C. R. Gibson Company
Printed in The United States of America
Library of Congress Catalog Card Number: 74-148610
SBN: 8378-1992-X

Paste
Picture
Here

My Beautiful Grandchild

Name _Alicia Jennifer Cherguin_
Born at _Northwest_ at _8:28 AM_.o'clock
Date _November 14, 1979_
Place _Northwest Hospital, Seattle_
Weight _8 lbs, 6 oz._ Length _21"_
Color of hair _dark brown_ Eyes _dark blue_
Parents _Lori & Kevin Cherguin_
Address _2916 W. Crockett_

They mailed out lots of tiny cards
To announce this baby's birth.
I would have used sky-writing
To tell *everyone* on earth!

Announcement

Paste Here

I hope I've heard only a rumor.
For surely it cannot be true
That just to keep peace
In the family
The baby was named after you!

Baby Was Named

_____

Reason Why

_____

_____

_____

_____

Paste Picture Here

The First Time

I knew the day
I saw this child
That here was Genius,
And I smiled.
For, from a family
So select,
It's only what
One should expect!

I Saw Baby

Paste
"Our" Picture
Here

Illustrious(?)Ancestors

_____

_____

_____

_____

_____

_____

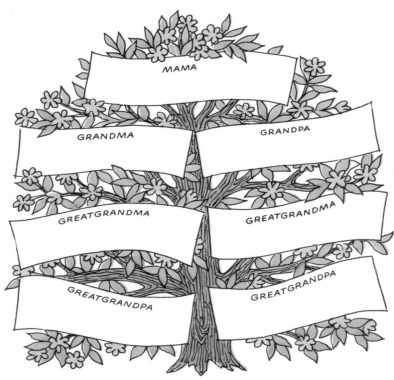

MAMA

GRANDMA   GRANDPA

GREATGRANDMA   GREATGRANDMA

GREATGRANDPA   GREATGRANDPA

Who Was Born

	Date
Mama_____	_____
Grandma_____	_____
Great Grandma_____	_____
Great Grandpa_____	_____
Grandpa_____	_____
Great Grandma_____	_____
Great Grandpa_____	_____

Where And When

Daddy_____ Date _____

Grandma_____ _____

Great Grandma_____ _____

Great Grandpa_____ _____

Grandpa_____ _____

Great Grandma_____ _____

Great Grandpa_____ _____

Mom And Dad

Paste Picture Here

Who does the baby
   resemble?
It's really quite
   easy to see.
Just study both Mom
   and Dad's faces
And then take a good
   look at me!

Baby's First Home

Address _____

_____

Paste Picture Here

She's calling everyone she's known
Since way back in her youth.
She thinks they're wild to hear the news:
Her grandchild has a tooth!

Baby's First Tooth

Other Important Firsts

Cute Tricks

Baby dumped the cereal bowl
And that was quite a trick!
So why should what the baby did
Make Mommy's head feel sick?

Funny Pics

GAMMY?

The fellow in the fireplace
Could turn out to be just Dad.
But who's the competition
That he didn't know he had?

Baby's First Christmas

Paste Picture Here

I have a funny feeling
And it stirs around in me
When I ask our Baby's mother
What the favorite toy might be.
I really shouldn't quiz her
For I fear that someday maybe
She'll forget and name a plaything
That *I* didn't give to Baby!

Favorite Toys

Likes And Dislikes

One candle for a birthday cake.
The year's gone by so soon!
And Baby's learned a lot of things . . .
Like how to use a spoon!

Baby's First Birthday

Height: Weight:

Paste Picture Here

Just A Few

Family Snapshots

Say,
Have you
Got a minute?
I don't
Like to brag,
But
I've a few
Pictures
Right here
In my bag . . .

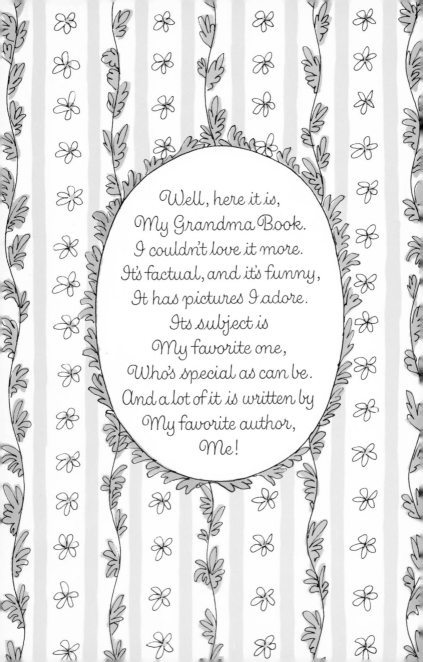

Well, here it is,
My Grandma Book.
I couldn't love it more.
It's factual, and it's funny,
It has pictures I adore.
Its subject is
My favorite one,
Who's special as can be.
And a lot of it is written by
My favorite author,
Me!